Courge is the Way!

Gabriele [illegible]

What people are saying about VUCA²

A pragmatic book for all those who want to choose the path of success in life...

Prof. Univ. Dr. Dumitru Constantin-Dulcan,
Bestselling author of *The Intelligence of Matter*

Your Beautiful Book Gave Me Great Energy and Inspiration.

Dr. Petra Müeller-Demary,
Founder of Solution Surfers® Romania

A practical and easy to implement guide that makes an extraordinary contribution to the world of wellness and wellbeing.

Walt Hampton, J.D., Founder & CEO
Summit Success, LLC, and bestselling
author of *Journeys on the Edge: Living A Life That Matters*

A wonderful guide for self examination to the path of authentic leadership.

Jennifer Povlitz, Division Director,
UBS Wealth Management

The book is really a practical guide that contributes to a state of wellbeing, stimulates inspiration, encourages the manifestation of vulnerability in a meaningful way in the life of the one who chooses to read it. A manifesto of courage, a gentle and clear encouragement at the same time. An avalanche of emotions with high vibrations. Thank you!

Stefania Dudau, Psychologist

A great, must read. Authentic content and contagiously motivational!

Ian Moldovan, PMP, CFM, FMP

I found in Gabriela's book the tools needed for a more orderly and clear life. Gabriela's advice comes from her own experience and from the soul of a warm and special woman whom I had the joy of meeting personally. It's a book that we should always have close to read or browse from time to time when we want a new perspective on a situation, when we want to put our thoughts and lives in order, when we want answers, but we do not know how to formulate the question. It is a book that brings us back to ourselves, allowing us to truly look at others and at the outside world. I highly recommend it!

Mihaela Oglinda, author of The Fitting Room

An inspirational book, a journey of self-understanding; convinced me that it is worth fighting for things that I may not have had the courage to think about until now. I believe that through her own experiences, the author manages to create a path that could be followed by all those who strive for a better self. Congratulations!

Mihaela Seciu, English Teacher

Very motivational and inspiring. I bought the book the moment I learned about it. Gabi is absolutely an amazing person and I love what she created in her book. Very motivational and easy to implement.

Mihaela Carsin, Ethics Senior Manager

Butterfly cover composition by the author, with much appreciated support from Matthew Cross and designer Tom Reczek, RZKDesign.com

Publishing Data

Published in the United States of America by Hoshin Media Group

P.O. Box 13, New Canaan, Connecticut 06840 USA

www.HoshinMedia.com

ISBN 978-1-939623-08-9

Tap The Power Within You

Gabriela Elena Blaga
Founder & CEO Innerpreneur.ro

Dedication

To my parents Arsinica and Ion from whom I learned the power of kindness, love, respect and humbleness.

To my sister Mihaela who has protected me since I was born.

Thank You! I love You!

No matter what name you use, no matter which way you choose, you will get somewhere. Life circumstances will lead you to some destination and you contribute to that, willingly or unwillingly, consciously or unconsciously. What might eventually matter is what you make of the life force inside you that supports and accompanies this travel into unpredictability, uncertainty and groundlessness.

Daniela Andreescu

CONTENTS

I. Foreword by Matthew K. Cross 7

II. Why I Wrote This Book and How You Could Use It 11

III. What Does VUCA Mean? 13

IV. $VUCA^2$ 17

V. $VUCA^2$ Questions 35

VI. Resources & Thank You 57

VII. Instead of Good Bye 67

About the Author 69

I

Foreword

Models and frameworks can equip you with the means to either open up your vision and horizon of possibilities or close them down. Enhanced perspective is the foundation for courageous and effective action—which leads you to better achieve and enjoy your full potential.

The world today exhibits increasing **Volatility**, **Uncertainty**, **Complexity** and **Ambiguity**—the acronym **VUCA**, originally coined by US military leaders and used in US Army War College training near the Cold War's end. It is based on Warren Bennis and Burt Nanus' work and perception of an increasingly VUCA world. It has since become a popular model for business thinking and action.

In this gem of a book, Gabriela Blaga introduces **VUCA^2**: a breakthrough booster rocket to the original VUCA model. **VUCA^2** compliments and balances VUCA, offering the synergy necessary to navigate the VUCA world with more clarity and confidence. It provides a golden door to your strengths to engage and impact your world.

Gabriela integrates the synergistic qualities of **Vulnerability**, **Uniqueness**, **Courage** and **Authenticity** to create VUCA^2's operational framework. Each has both a direct and a subtle power which supports seeing and seizing opportunities with greater flow and fortune.

VUCA	VUCA²
Volatility, Uncertainty, Complexity, Ambiguity	**Vulnerability, Uniqueness, Courage, Authenticity**
More outside-in, reactive	More inside-out, pre/proactive
Threats, challenges	Strengths, opportunities
More contractive	More expansive
Left brain, thinking, analysis	Right brain, feeling, synthesis

VUCA² is a heart-based approach to address and engage people, opportunities, problems or challenges. It is valuable to assess threats and plan for worst-case scenarios—to engage the original VUCA's Volatility, Uncertainty, Complexity and Ambiguity in any crucial situation. Yet such efforts are greatly enhanced by starting with VUCA². Having your inner sight and strengths clarified and boosted first gives you a secret weapon—which boosts outer world focused planning and action. I especially enjoy how Gabriela invites you into VUCA² with her provocative questions.

I predict the benefits you'll enjoy from Gabriela's gift will include elevated *insight, action and results*:

- Enhanced **insight** on your strengths, path and purpose
- More flowing and impactful **action**
- Greater **results** in your endeavors, personal and professional

I salute you on your adventure ahead. Cheers as you tap your VUCA² Power!

Matthew Cross
CEO & Founder • LeadershipAlliance.com

Foreword

Why I Wrote This Book and How You Could Use It

This book is a gift for all of YOU who have the courage to live authentically and pay attention to the imprint you leave in this Volatile, Uncertain, Complex and Ambiguous (VUCA) world.

I also wrote this book as a celebration of the kilometers I've traveled so far through Life. It intertwines personal stories with elements of my leadership coaching practice. It is also the vehicle through which I launch a new concept in coaching, **VUCA^2: Vulnerability, Uniqueness, Courage and Authenticity**.

What was the day I first thought of writing this book? I don't remember exactly... I know, however, that I wrote its name on a blank page in a beautiful agenda in July 2019. As fate would have it, this book wanted to come out in the very challenging year of 2020. Initially I imagined it would be oriented more towards my life story. The form you are reading now emerged at the end of August 2020, after one of many inspirational conversations with my beloved man—with whom I grow and realize, more than ever, that ***Life is Love and Love is Life!***

You can read this book in at least three different ways:

1. Page by page, in chronological order.
2. Begin with the VUCA^2 questions followed by my personal stories.
3. Start anywhere you feel like and take it from there...

Whichever way you choose, I am confident my words will be received with openness and joy by at least 1,979 people.

What Does VUCA Mean?

The acronym VUCA was first used in 1991 by the U.S. Army War College, based on the leadership theories developed by Warren Bennis and Burt Nanus in their book *Leaders: The Strategies for Taking Charge.* The United States Military started using VUCA to describe and provide a framework to better navigate an increasingly turbulent world.

I first heard of VUCA during my corporate life in 2014. The term is used to describe an **environment characterized by:**

- **V**olatility: Change is rapid and unpredictable in its nature and extent.
- **U**ncertainty: The present is unclear, and the future is uncertain.
- **C**omplexity: Many different, interconnected factors come into play, with the potential to cause chaos and confusion.
- **A**mbiguity: There is a lack of clarity or awareness about situations.

**from www.mindtools.com/pages/article/managing-vuca-world.htm*

A VUCA environment can:

- Destabilize people, cause anxiety and decrease motivation.
- Endanger careers.
- Paralyze and degrade decision-making processes.
- Jeopardize projects and long-term innovation.
- Overwhelm people and organizations.

On the next page is a short exercise to give you a taste of the original VUCA model.

Mini VUCA Exercise

1. **What's a situation you'd like to better understand or improve:**

2. **Briefly describe this situation through the VUCA lens. Then add an insight addressing each VUCA word.**

How Is Your Chosen Situation:

Volatile?

How can you calm things down

Uncertain?

What ARE you certain about, especially the positive

Complex? ____________________

____

____

____

What key aspect can you simplify ____________________

____

____

____

Ambiguous? ____________________

____

____

____

How can you enhance clarity ____________________

____

____

____

While preparing a presentation for the Professional Women's Network Romania, inspiration visited me and whispered a remedy that we can use to better live in these VUCA times:

$VUCA^2$ = Vulnerability + Uniqueness + Courage + Authenticity

Using $VUCA^2$ we can face the challenges presented by the VUCA world with increased agility and assertiveness.

$VUCA^2$ = Vulnerability + Uniqueness + Courage + Authenticity

Have the courage to follow your heart and intuition. They somehow already know what you truly want to become. Everything else is secondary.

Steve Jobs

We are born, we learn, we love, we create...

We are born, we learn to love, we learn to create... So many meanings! But in order to understand them, it is necessary to *remain painfully open.*

I chose to stay *painfully open* from that very day on a Monday, (March 19th, 1979), when I was born (now you know why I mentioned 1,979 people before ☺)

I decided that it would be good to start my life journey in a small provincial town, located between the vineyards and Vrancea Mountains in Romania: Panciu (pronounced "Pahn-choo").

My parents named me Gabriela Elena, and if I had been a boy (as I found out was my father's wish), I would have been named Lucian, in honor of Lucian Blaga (see next page)—with whom I feel related.

The child laughs: Wisdom and love are my play!
The young man sings: Playing and wisdom are my love!
The old man is silent: Love and play are my wisdom!

Lucian Blaga

__Lucian Blaga__ was the greatest creative personality in Romanian culture in the twentieth century. His work—as a poet, philosopher, essayist, playwright and translator of poetry—is a personal synthesis of great originality, deep ethnic inspiration, fueled by an amazing openness to the most varied aspects of the human spirit: philosophy and science, history and religion, and especially the complex and controversial field of arts. The adversities Blaga faced during his life are better perceived if we consider that in the 1950s, when he was nominated for the Nobel Prize, the Romanian authorities of the time did not allow him to respond to the invitation made by the Royal Swedish Academy.

I felt the touch of creativity and curiosity at the age of four when I asked my mother why I was not born as a flower or why the table is not called a chair, and vice-versa... the playful imagination of a child. I had no idea then that in the years to come, I would use the infinite power of questions in my coaching, journalism and creative pursuits. I also remember the answer I gave to the question "What do you want to become when you grow up?" My answer: Educator. Looking back, I wasn't far from the truth.

As a child, I increased my vitamin "C"—creativity + curiosity—through reading + writing. I remember with joy the top grade I received during a Romanian language and literature contest when I was nine. The award-winning "masterpiece" was a short composition about the beauty of the sky, which was the moving canvas for my imagination from my earliest memories. I remember endlessly looking for characters in the shapes of the clouds. Today, looking at the sky is my free-of-charge exercise of meditation and inspiration, available at any time. The main ingredient is full presence.

In his book ***The School for Gods***, Stefano Elio D'Anna shared this evocative thought:

Look, it's a full moon. Throughout life, people can see a thousand full moons, but it is very possible that at the end of their lives they realized that they did not have time to observe any.

I was an introverted child, spending hours reading or playing with my family of dolls.

I could have spent weeks in a corner of the house surrounded by my favorite books. Later in life I became what I am today: an ambivert.

My studies in high school focused on economics. I would have gone to an English French high school to feed my passion for languages, if I hadn't felt it would have been a financial burden for my parents. So, I chose economics and stayed in my small town, guarded by a boulevard of chestnut trees. I then continued my studies in accounting in Iasi (the capital of one of the four historic regions of Romania, pronounced *Yah-shh*), following in the footsteps of my sister Mihaela.

Many years have passed since my walks on Copou Hill, near my university. I lived experiences that brought me closer and closer to me and met people who, in one way or another, were my guides. Some accompanied me for a while, others chose to leave, others for whom I am grateful are by my side and support me with much love.

Love is the most difficult and dangerous form of courage. Courage is the most desperate, admirable, and noble kind of love.

Delmore Schwartz

In 2001 I decided to move to Bucharest, the capital. For the next fifteen years I had several interesting roles in Fortune 500 companies, where I worked with people from all over the world. I've learned much about what differentiates us and brings us closer together, regardless of culture, age or position.

My work included coordinating an array of large global projects in multiple countries. My various roles afforded a unique window into our individual and organizational **Vulnerabilities, Uniqueness, Courage, Authenticity** and desire for productive harmony. **This was the origin of VUCA².**

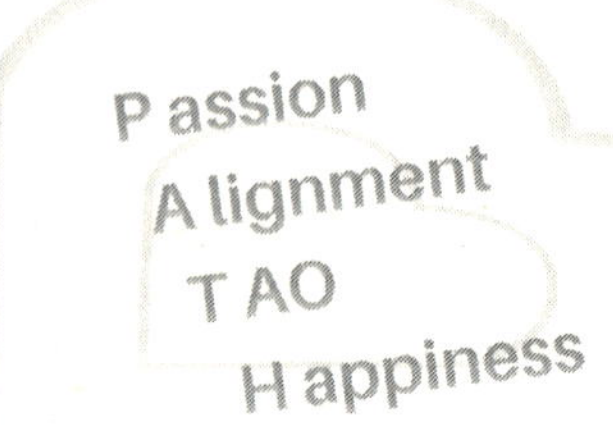

innerpreneur.

In 2018, my path came into clearer focus, and I incorporated on an emotional, physical, and mental level my purpose—what Sir Ken Robinson calls one's *Element*.

At that time, I was beginning a new life cycle rich in feelings, experiences, discoveries and an unexpected departure: on July 3 of that year, my Dad left this world and became my guardian angel.

Thus 2018 was the gateway for what followed.

It is difficult to express in words how I felt when I discovered and sensed my true calling—it felt like butterflies all over my body! I won't go any further until I tell you the story of how the butterfly became my personal symbol. It was not by accident; it came to me in the form of a drawing.

In the winter of 2014, I was recovering from a serious health challenge in Copenhagen where I was also based at the time. One day as I was rebuilding my strength, I drew a butterfly. I called Hope, through my childhood eyes. My metamorphosis began...

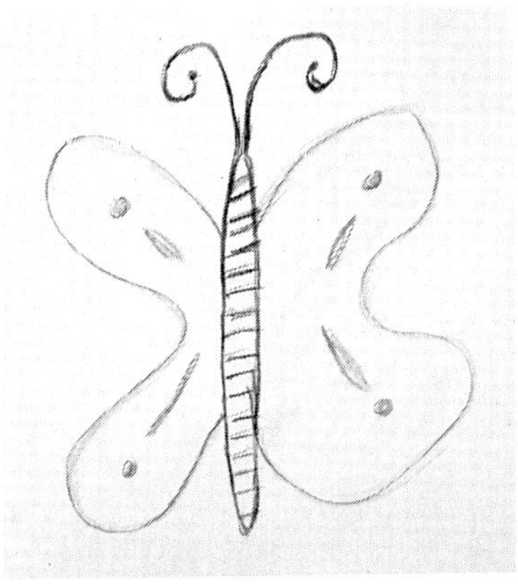

I drew a second butterfly, this time in watercolor, in the summer of 2014 while on a mindfulness retreat in Tuscany.

A butterfly's metamorphosis, with its four phases is how I define my inner journey which began in 2013. Everything I have experienced since then has come to me at just the right time, feeding me with the life and love nutrients needed for my own metamorphosis.

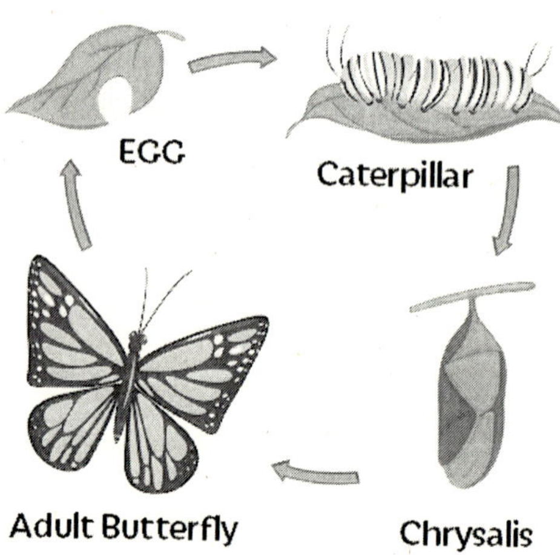

Our soul's sense of place is our own AUTHENTICITY. But we don't arrive to this Earth on a straight path. We have to go through many lessons and transformations before we become a butterfly.

CoachingCafeClub.com

I don't think there's a general recipe for discovering one's life path. I feel our authentic path reveals itself in the moment when you begin to love yourself deeply—and know WHO YOU ARE. In my case, it was the moment I understood that vulnerability is both my anchor *and* my lighthouse. Vulnerability gives me great strength, inspiration and power. There was a time when I considered Vulnerability to be a weakness—yet it became the key that activated my Courage.

When your true identity is revealed and you fully embrace it, you know when a person, a job or any situation is not beneficial for you—and you have the Courage to avoid it--or leave. You have the courage, even if some might call you arrogant, to say directly what you want and to stop compromising.

No need to tell you that your time on Earth is limited, for you who have chosen to open the pages of this book understand how important it is to honor every minute, hour and day of this precious gift called Life.

VULNERABILITY

When we were children, we used to think that when we were grown-up we would no longer be vulnerable. But to grow up is to accept vulnerability... To be alive is to be vulnerable.

Madeleine L'Engle

What does "Vulnerability" mean to me?

It's the ability to open up to life and people, even at the risk of being hurt.

It would be good to understand, once and for all, that vulnerability is a force which:

- *Allows us to feel more connected to other people, and thus cultivate healthy connections.*
- *Helps us improve our relationships, allowing us to be more emotionally available.*

- *Enables us to be more authentic and honest with ourselves and others.*
- *Opens doors that would have remained closed if we had not allowed ourselves to be fully open.*
- *Promotes general well-being, allowing us to experience wholeheartedly, with presence, all that life has to offer.*

I am a firm believer that when you choose to integrate and honor your vulnerability you will feel connected to what is essential for your personal identity, purpose and well-being. And this will help you to reach the meeting point between your passions and skills, the "personal element" as Sir Ken Robinson called it in his genius book *The Element*.

In *The Icarus Deception: How High Will You Fly*, Seth Godin says,

> *The path we have at hand tells us to allow human nature to come to the surface, make art, and fly much higher than we were told it would be possible.*

I believe we see this path only if we recognize and learn to accept our vulnerabilities, even if at first, we might feel a deep fear. As Joseph Campbell said:

> *The cave you are afraid to enter may hide the treasure you are looking for.*

I am quite curious by nature, hence some months ago I conducted a quiz asking my network to share their feelings and beliefs about vulnerability. Their answers were both provocative and touching.

- *To wear your wounds with pride, like a warrior facing life; to see those wounds as your own strength.*
- *Be benevolent, forgiving.*
- *Vulnerability carries us into an inner process of self-knowledge. It means becoming aware of who we are, what we have and can lose and what we can become or gain, once we understand the mental and emotional limits we can overcome.*
- *I think vulnerability is my best friend. By becoming aware of it, accepting it and learning from it about myself, I evolve beautifully.*
- *Know what things can hurt or make you sad. To trust that it is worth letting your loved ones find out what can hurt you.*
- *For me, being vulnerable means opening your soul to people, whether they are close friends or strangers. Ask for help when you need it, without being afraid that you will be refused or that there will be no one to help you. To love, to hope, to believe.*
- *To cry in front of others, to open my soul when it's hard for me.*
- *Vulnerability is the normal state many of us have unfortunately lost in order to adapt to the digital world.*
- *To be vulnerable, for me, is to give up control and let your guard down.*

UNIQUENESS

Always remember that you are absolutely unique. Just like everyone else.

Margaret Mead

By owning your vulnerability, you can manifest your **Uniqueness**. This is how every nuance of your personality can come fully into the light. The harmonious interweaving of the unique qualities with which each of us comes into the world supports our living in a VUCA world.

We are all unique and we contribute to the best and the worst in the world. It is worth treating yourself and others as precious beings! **The more we grow and share this spirit, the healthier the space between and within us will become—and we nurture well-being for all.**

COURAGE

Courage is the only virtue you cannot fake.

Nassim Taleb

In these times, many feel an increasing and tremendous pressure from the environment we live in. It is a period which brings up big fears; some new and some familiar. I believe that fear is an inevitable emotion in our lives, which often appears whenever change happens—whether internal or external.

We best not run from our fears. Instead, we ought to dare to dialogue with fear, to understand what it wants to tell us, to tame it using the method the fox suggests to The Little Prince in the book of the same title by legendary aviator and author Antoine de Saint-Exupery:

> *You have to be very patient, the fox said. At first, you'll sit a little further away from me in the grass. I will look at you out of the corner of my eye, and you will not say a word. Speaking is a source of misunderstanding. But you will be able to sit closer and closer to me every day.*

My life experience has taught me to dialogue with my fears; to listen to and understand them. In the process I gained a transformative gift: **COURAGE**.

What does courage mean to some of the beautiful people I know? How do they define courage? What is the bravest thing we can do in life? I asked and they answered!

- *To love - period. Again!*
- *Always try new things; take risks; keep your promises, face your own demons, own your shadows.*
- *Courage means exploration. You evaluate the risks and prepare yourself as best you can and then venture into the unknown.*
- *Courage is a muscle we have to exercise. It is vital to strengthen your courage by doing all the things that you are afraid of and dream of in silence.*
- *Courage is expressing your values when others are not aligned with them, especially living in a world where the principle of „if you don't agree with me, you're against me" often seems to be the rule.*
- *Courage is when you speak your mind even though you know you might be judged. When you move forward regardless of the obstacles in your way; when you fight to protect others, no matter the consequences.*

- *Courage is being authentic today in a copy-paste world.*
- *Courage means trying things that may be beyond you, saying things that are hidden and trying to change something.*

It is said that you need courage to do what you love. It is also said that when you choose to do what you love, the Universe will support you and bring you the opportunities, the circumstances and the people you need. Yes, the Universe really works for you when you embrace your dreams and start building from them. Of course, during the journey, fear will appear—but DARE nonetheless!

The Universe is conspiring
to shower you with blessings.

Rob Brezsny
www.freewillastrology.com

AUTHENTICITY

Authenticity is a collection of choices that we have to make every day. It's about the choice to show up and be real. The choice to be honest. The choice to let our true selves be seen.

Brene Brown

Here is my acrostic for the words I associate authenticity with:

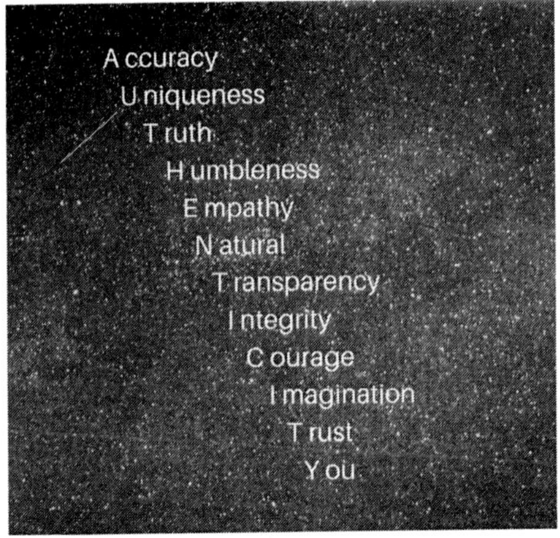

These words distill the authentic Ego which Brene speaks of.

I invite you to read what other people have shared when I asked what authenticity means for them:

- *Authenticity means honoring my soul. To be authentic means to stop and ask myself, "How do I feel? What would I really like to do?"*
- *What you say and what you do are consistent and there are no discrepancies between the two.*

- *Authenticity means the courage to be and live-in full understanding and harmony with yourself in this world. It means taking responsibility for and owning your life story.*
- *Being honest with yourself and those around you.*
- *Being aware of your personal values and living in accordance with them. This is not always easy, but it is definitely healthy!*
- *Authenticity means saying that even though you don't know who you will be tomorrow, today you feel like doing it and you will do it.*
- *Authenticity means knowing / (re)knowing your values and proving them in what you say and do.*
- *Authenticity, for me, means generosity and simplicity.*
- *I strongly link authenticity with sincerity, with honesty.*
- *It's a delicate subject. For me, authenticity means not deviating from your story. And in your story, to put much, much, much passion!*
- *Inner strength and faith.*
- *The freedom to express myself in all my beauty and glory!*

In an increasingly ***Volatile, Uncertain, Complex and Ambiguous environment,*** **Authenticity** is the foundation on which healthy connections and relationships are built—both personal and professional. An easy yet profound way to restore and embrace our authenticity is to learn from its natural practitioners: **Children!**

Children 'get it!'
They cry when they are hurt.
Squeal in delight when they are happy.
Children express their true feelings.
Connect to the child in YOU!

Lee Horbachewski

VUCA² Questions

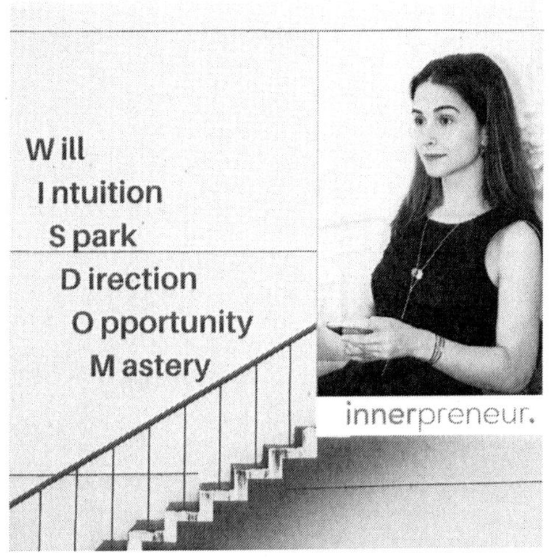

The questions contain the answers we seek.

Matthew Cross

Almost every day we are searching for answers to life's seemingly endless questions. We can train and sharpen our VUCA² using a set of 21 specific questions I created to help you bring VUCA² to life. **Feel free to write as little or as much as you like. Quality first; Quantity if it calls you.**

After 2 – 3 months, it wlll be useful to return to your initial answers to the questions and see if you'd answer differently with the perspective of time. Write down any new answers or insights if so.

1. **When was the last time you faced Uncertainty with Bravery?**

2. What do you associate with Vulnerability?

3. What are the main messages around Vulnerability in your workplace?

4. What do you fear the most?

5. On a scale of 1 to 10, 1 being lowest and 10 being highest, what is your comfort level with Vulnerability?

1 2 3 4 5 6 7 8 9 10

6. How does Vulnerability feel for you emotionally?

7. How do you feel when you share your personal story?

8. How do you define Authenticity?

9. Have you ever felt like an imposter in any part of your life?

9a. If so, when and why?

10. How would you define Courage?

11. When was the last time when you thought you were Courageous?

12. What gave you Courage then?

13. On a scale of 1 (low) to 10 (high), how Courageous are you feeling right NOW?

1 2 3 4 5 6 7 8 9 10

13a. What could you do from this level of personal Courage?

14. What are some of your Unique super-powers?

14a. When was the last time you used them?

15. Imagine you are watching a movie about the next 7 years of your life, what are some of the main scenes you'd like to see?

15a. From the scenes you saw above, which one lights you up the most and why?

16. In these Volatile, Uncertain, Complex and Ambiguous times (VUCA), what have you discovered about yourself that you didn't know?

17. Choose the first color that comes to mind for the VUCA² words:

Vulnerability ______________________________

Uniqueness ______________________________

Courage ______________________________

Authenticity ______________________________

18. Using the colors you've just selected, draw a picture or even a simple symbol that represents you now:

19. From the four VUCA² qualities select the ONE you'd most like to strengthen in your life at this time:

Circle one:

Vulnerability

Uniqueness

Courage

Authenticity

19a. Now, select one of the remaining three VUCA² qualities which would boost the quality you chose above to strengthen:

Circle one:

Vulnerability

Uniqueness

Courage

Authenticity

19b. Write your two choices below:

____________________ + ____________________

Your chosen VUCA² quality to strengthen	Your VUCA² booster quality

20. For the two VUCA² qualities you chose on the opposite page, write down 1 to 3 actions you will do starting today to strengthen them for the coming one or two months:

1. ______________________________

   ____

2. ______________________________

   ____

3. ______________________________

   ____

We've come to the end of our VUCA² journey.

I wish you much inspiration and joy in playing with the VUCA² diamond in your life.

Thank you for the precious time you invested in reading these pages. I dare to believe that you will take away at least three learnings from this book.

I wrote it with a lot of joy and with a rainbow of emotions. I often wondered, in the many days of writing," Who am I to come up with new perspectives around Vulnerability, Uniqueness, Courage and Authenticity...?" And my answer was:

> *I am one of the 7.8 billion people on Earth who undertook the opportunity to speak about those personal powers that help us to live more connected with one another, to create and maintain healthy connections with everything within and around us.*

Embracing my own vulnerability was possible thanks to the people I interacted with from 1979 until now.

Special thanks go to several people I dream of meeting with in this life: Brene Brown, Elizabeth Gilbert, Marie Forleo, Simon Sinek, Seth Godin...

I have been inspired by and feel a deep connection with Audrey Hepburn and Queen Marie of Romania, Sir Ken Robinson and Steve Jobs.

My deepest gratitude to the many people of light who offered / offer me their time and resources to grow together.

Thank you Edit for your support and encouragement from the first day we met.

Thank you Dr. Robert Friedman, for your caring insights and suggestions.

Thank you Cotroceni, my beloved neighborhood in Bucharest, for the creative energy gifted since 2018.

Thank you Matthew for your love, guidance and encouragement in writing this book and beyond.

Until next time, I hug you wholehearted.

Ella Blaga
Bucharest, September 2020

P.S. Please feel free to share any of your insights from this book at: COR@Innerpreneur.ro

I am always happy to engage around these topics and provide added guidance.

RESOURCES

People who reflect the VUCA² spirit and some of their quotes which inspire me:

Audrey Hepburn

Nothing it is impossible; the word itself says I'm possible!

Queen Marie of Romania

Nothing's far when one wants to get there.

Brene Brown

Vulnerability is the birthplace of love, belonging, joy, courage, empathy, and creativity. It is the source of hope, empathy, accountability, and authenticity. If we want greater clarity in our purpose or deeper and more meaningful spiritual lives, vulnerability is the path.

Ken Robinson

Life is not linear, it is organic. We create our lives symbiotically as we explore our talents in relation to the circumstances, they help create for us.

Steve Jobs

Your time is limited, so don't waste it living someone else's life. Don't be trapped by dogma—which is living with the results of other people's thinking. Don't let the noise of others' opinions drown out your own inner voice. And most important, have the courage to follow your heart and intuition.

Elizabeth Gilbert

Let people have their opinions. More than that—let people love their opinions, just as you and I are in love with ours. But never delude yourself into believing that you require someone else's blessing (or even their comprehension) in order to make your own creative work. And always remember that people's judgments about you are none of your business.

Philippe Petit

Believe in the miracles that exist around you, inside others, in you. Go look for them. Feed your imagination. In this way, build your destiny.

Jordan B. Peterson

To stand up straight with your shoulders back is to accept the terrible responsibility of life, with eyes wide open. It means deciding to voluntarily transform the chaos of potential into the realities of habitable order. It means adopting the burden of self-conscious vulnerability and accepting the end of the unconscious paradise of childhood, where finitude and mortality are only dimly comprehended. It means willingly undertaking the sacrifices necessary to generate a productive and meaningful reality (it means acting to please God, in the ancient language).

John F. Kennedy

The Chinese use two brush strokes to write the word 'crisis.' One brush stroke stands for danger: the other for opportunity. In a crisis, be aware of the danger--but recognize the opportunity.

Alan Watts

The only way to make sense out of change is to plunge into it, move with it, and join the dance.

Viktor E. Frankl

When we are no longer able to change a situation, we are challenged to change ourselves.

Some Favorite Inspirational Books

Antoine de Saint-Exupery – *The Little Prince*

Mihaly Csikszentmihalyi – *Flow*

Brene Brown – *Daring Greatly, Dare to Lead*

Elizabeth Gilbert – *Big Magic*

Carol S. Dweck – *Mindset*

Jordan B. Peterson – *12 Rules For Life*

Sir Ken Robinson – *Finding Your Element*

Daniela Andreescu – *The Gift of Now*

Scott Harison – *Thirst: A Story of Redemption, Compassion, and a Mission to Bring Clean Water to the World*

Seth Godin – *The Icarus Deception: How High Will You Fly*

Matthew K. Cross – *The Millionaire's Map, The Hoshin North Star process*

Nassim Nicholas Taleb – *Antifragile, Skin in the Game*

Julia Cameron – *The Artist's Way*

Clarissa Pinkola Estes – *Women Who Run with the Wolves: Myths and Stories of the Wild Woman Archetype*

Elio D'Anna – *The School of Gods*

Alan Watts – *The Wisdom of Insecurity: A Message for an Age of Anxiety, Become what You are*

Viktor K. Frankl – *Man' Search for Meaning*

Desmond Tutu, Dalai Lama – *The Book of Joy*

Ryan Holiday – *The Obstacle Is the Way: The Timeless Art of Turning Trials into Triumph*

Alex Beard – *Natural Born Learners*

Some Favorite Inspirational Websites, Videos

The Book of Life
https://www.theschooloflife.com/thebookoflife/

The Power of Vulnerability | Brené Brown
https://www.youtube.com/watch?v=iCvmsMzlF7o&t=68s

Listening to Shame | Brené Brown
https://www.youtube.com/watch?v=psN1DORYYV0

Elizabeth Gilbert & Marie Forleo on Fear, Authenticity and Big Magic
https://www.youtube.com/watch?v=HyUYa-BnjU8&t=2s

Philippe Petit: The Journey Across the High Wire
https://www.youtube.com/watch?v=k3zZVQPaKKQ&t=34s

Blow Up Your Bridge | Matthew K. Cross | TEDxBaiaMare
https://www.youtube.com/watch?v=k4VeWyOylk4&t=3s

Despre Puterea Emoției | Oana Pellea | TEDxCluj
https://www.youtube.com/watch?v=VLVmOxbYuZc&t=3s

One year ago during a coaching program within a corporation, I met Alexandra Mureșan. Coaching her I learned how creative and brave she is! I invited Alexandra to share with us what VUCA² means to her and also to enchant our eyes and souls with two of her paintings.

Trying to describe what vulnerability, uniqueness, courage and authenticity mean to me I realized that I can't talk about one without the other.

For me, vulnerability means compassion for myself and others. Not everyone has the courage to be imperfect. We are all trying to show that we live a fulfilled and happy life—but it is difficult to admit that we are fragile, make wrong decisions and are often not good with others.

There are rare occasions when I think of myself as being brave and I continue to risk being loved, accepted, rejected. There are times when I feel braver and I dare to do more. I try to discover my talents and be authentic through my imprint on the universe.

Instead of Good Bye

Create whatever causes a revolution in your heart.

Elizabeth Gilbert

innerpreneur.

DREAM is an *acrostic*—and if you reached this page I am convinced you've noticed some others ☺. I love playing with words through acrostics and I use them in my coaching practice as well.

An acrostic is a poem, word puzzle, or other composition in which certain letters in each line form a word or words.

\- Oxford Dictionary

Now, it's your turn:

Create an acrostic for your first name. Then, share it with a good friend / lover ☺ Then ask your friend / lover to create an acrostic for your name. What are your insights from this playful exercise?

About the Author

Gabriela Elena Blaga is founder and CEO of INNERPRENEUR S.R.L., a boutique consulting firm based in Bucharest, Romania. She facilitates healthy profitability, growth and sustainability of people and organizations through creative project management, solution focus coaching, mentoring and storytelling.

In her 10+ years working in Fortune 500 companies, Gabriela collaborated closely with people and teams from all over the world. Her work has included coordinating an array of large global projects in multiple countries such as the UK, Switzerland, Russia, Ukraine, Costa Rica, Hungary, Turkey, the Czech Republic and Romania. Her various roles afforded a unique window into individual and organizational vulnerabilities, courage and the universal desire for productive harmony. Gabriela is a mentor in Professional Women's Network Romania and contributing writer for *Pagina de Psihologie* (*Page of Psychology*). A former co-producer and moderator of the BiziLive TV program *Tell Me Your Story*, she's also a gifted journalist. This is her first book.

Gabriela is available for interviews, presentations and coaching. Contact her at: COR@Innerpreneur.ro

Picture credits:
Butterfly life cycle:
sites.google.com/site/lepidobutterfliesofsrilanka/life-cycle-of-butterfly

All other pictures and acrostics: Author's collection.

ALSO FROM HOSHIN MEDIA

The Hoshin North Star Process™

by Matthew K. Cross

Chart your way to total success with the strategic alignment process of the world's greatest companies. 86 pages, illustrated workbook.

The Golden Ratio & Fibonacci Sequence

by Matthew K. Cross & Robert D. Friedman, M.D.

A delightful introduction and primer to the golden keys to genius, health, wealth & excellence. 62 pages, richly illustrated in color.

Nature's Secret Nutrient™

by Robert D. Friedman, M.D. & Matthew K. Cross

Breakthrough playbook for PEAK health & longevity. Ventures boldly into new territory where no doctor, nutritionist or personal trainer has gone before. 500 pages, richly illustrated.

The Genius Activation Quote Book

by Matthew K. Cross & Robert D. Friedman, M.D.

Activate your innate genius with thought-provoking Golden Ratio quotes. 134 pages, illustrated.

The Millionaire's MAP™

by Matthew K. Cross

Chart your way to abundance by tapping the power of your imagination via the Fibonacci Sequence, Nature's secret design and growth code. 144 pages, illustrated workbook.

The Little Book of Romanian Wisdom

by Diana Doroftei & Matthew K. Cross

#1 bestseller in category. Discover the unique, wonderfully inspiring wisdom of Romania. 184 pages, illustrated; in English and Romanian.